The Adventures of Troy
Home Again
Book 4

Written and Illustrated by

Hope Kelley

Copyright 2025 by Hope Kelley

Original Story/Text and Original Art/Illustrations

The Adventures of Troy Home Again

By Hope Kelley

Early Learners Series Book 4

For Author Book Signings and Art Exhibits:

www.HopeKelley.com

For Book Publishing:

www.HopeKelleyBookPublishing.com

Printed in the United States of America

All rights reserved solely by the author. The author guarantees all contents are original and do not infringe upon the legal rights of any other person or work. No part of this book may be reproduced in any form without the permission of the author. The views expressed in this book are not necessarily those of the publisher.

"I lovingly dedicate this book to
my precious newborn grandson,
Lando.
Look forward to watching you
grow up into a caring man just
like your father. So many
fun and exciting times ahead.

Your adoring Grammie,
Hope Kelley

Troy was once again headed to the farm to see all of his friends, just like he had been doing for the past few years. He loved this time of the day when the sun was shining high in the sky.

He enjoyed seeing the beautiful swan family swimming in the **tranquil** pond below. Troy loved the springtime, and he happily flew to the farm just about every day.

As Troy flew over the *grazing field* for the sheep, he was surprised there was no one was around.

"The sheep and the two working dogs must be in the south field today," Troy thought to himself.

At that very moment, Troy had a memory of the very first time he **stumbled** into the farm when he was just a baby. He had fallen out of the nest he shared with his twin brother, Balde. The storm had carried him far from his home. It would be awhile before his family would find him again.

The sweet mother hen had taken pity on him and let him follow her and her baby chicks for awhile. He loved her for being so kind to him back then.

Troy got to the farm and found his two new friends, Darcy and Belle, hanging out with his old friend, Maggie the horse.

Darcy was a very nice *gentleman* pup. He was always ready to help anyone who needed him.

The black blue-eyed pup was Belle, and she was born on the farm. Her mother was Troy's old friend, Bella. He missed Bella. She was sent to another farm to help with the sheep.

"Hi, Troy!" said Darcy.

"Hello, Troy!" What are you up to this nice day?" said Belle.

"Just wanted to come by and say hello to my friends!" said Troy.

As Troy flew away to go home, he saw a pretty eagle coming in his direction.

"Wow!" Troy thought to himself.

"I wonder who she is?"

They flew past one another and looked back and smiled, and continued on their way. Troy had never seen such a beautiful eagle.

Darcy watched as the eagle, Aliana, flew over the farm.

He had seen her **soaring** around the farm a few times, so he thought she must have a home in a tree not far away.

Now back at his home tree, Troy could not stop thinking about the beautiful eagle.

"I wonder if she lives in a tree nearby. He was hoping to see her again soon.

A little later that day, Aliana was also *ruminating* about Troy as she sat in her home tree.

"I wonder who he is?" Aliana thought. "Maybe he will be flying around the farm or countryside again tomorrow?" Just like Troy, she was hoping to see him again soon.

The next day, the skies were looking like it might rain. Troy was heading back to the farm to see his friends. He saw Darcy and Belle in the field **herding** the sheep.

"Hello, Troy," Darcy said to the eagle.

"Hi, Troy!" Belle barked up to greet him.

Troy said, "I saw a pretty eagle with pink feathers yesterday."

"I've seen her flying around here, too," Darcy said.

"I hope I see her again," Troy responded.

"Let's go to the wishing tree and make a wish so you will see her again, Troy!" Belle said.

"Good idea!" Troy responded.

A little later in the day when the sheep were back in their pens,

the three friends set out to visit the wishing tree. It was far away from the farm, and it would be a little *journey* to get there. Troy would make his wish there to see Aliana again.

Coincidentally, at this very moment, Aliana was at the wishing tree making a wish of her own. She sat in the tree and made a wish to find Troy, and hoped it wouldn't take too long.

Troy, Darcy, and Belle were enjoying their adventure going to see the wishing tree. As they got to the covered bridge, the rain started falling. They would *remain* under the bridge until the rain passed.

By the time they got to the wishing tree, Aliana had already left. Little did the friends know she had been here a few minutes earlier.

Darcy said, "Go ahead, Troy. Make your wish!"

Not knowing her name, Troy said out loud, "I hope to see the pretty eagle with the pink feathers very soon!"

Darcy and Belle made their way back to the farm, and Troy headed to his home nest. It had gotten late, and the full moon was brightly *guiding* his way home.

The next day, Troy saw his good friend, Maurice the Cat, down by the stream. The pretty black farm cat, Drackie, was with him.

"Hey, Maurice!" said Troy.

'Hi, Troy! I want you to meet Drackie," Darcy said as he **introduced** the cat.

"Hi, Drackie!" Troy responded.

Troy continued, "By any chance, have you seen the eagle with pink feathers lately?"

"I have seen her around, but not today," Maurice said.

"Okay, see you later," Troy responded as he flew away.

"Goodbye, Troy!" shouted Maurice and Drackie.

Troy was **confident** he would see the eagle again.

Troy decided he would go to the horse field and visit Stetson. Maybe he had seen the eagle today.

"Hi, Stetson," Troy said as he flew down and perched on the fence.

Stetson trotted over to him and said, "Hey, Troy."

"I was wondering if you have seen the eagle with pink feathers today?" Troy asked.

"I'm afraid not, Troy. I'm sorry," Stetson responded ***sincerely*** in his low husky voice.

"Okay, well… see you later!" Troy said as he flew away.

"Bye, Troy!"

Troy was **downcast** as he made his way back to his home tree.

"Where could she be?" Troy wondered. He hoped the wishing tree was going to grant his wish to see her again.

The next day, Troy set out to **search** for the eagle once again. He was hoping he would see her and find out her name. That would be a nice start.

As he approached the farm he saw Darcy and Belle lying in the spring flowers.

Before Troy could say anything, Darcy yelled up to him and said, "No, Troy, we haven't seen her today!"

Troy laughed and said, "I guess you both know what is on my mind!"

Darcy and Belle laughed with him.

Darcy says, "You've been like this for days!"

Darcy flew by the horse field and saw Maggie and Stetson.

"No, we haven't see her, Troy!"

Maggie and Stetson said in *unison.*

Once again, Troy laughed and continued on his way.

A few months went by and then suddenly, one crisp *autumn* day, Troy was flying by the old church and saw her! His wish had finally come true!

Troy flew up to her and said, " Hello, I'm Troy. I'm so happy to see you again."

She responded, I'm Aliana. I'm happy to see you again, too."

Troy and Aliana spent a lot of time flying around together the next few days. Troy took her by the farm to introduce her to his friends but there was no one around. They would come back another day.

The two eagles were so happy they had found each other. They spent many days flying around and seeing new and *picturesque* places. Troy had found his mate. He already loved Aliana so much!

One day, Troy took Aliana to the farm to meet his friends.

They were all *ecstatic* to see Troy and to meet Aliana. She now had a lot of new friends!

Troy would no longer be living in his home tree alone.

Troy and Aliana made their nest in Troy's home tree. They were now ***eagerly*** awaiting their baby eagles to hatch and be born. Troy was about to be a father and Aliana would soon become a mother. With great patience, Troy's wish for a family had come true. Troy was finally home again!

The End

Do you remember the names of Troy and Aliana's friends?

Darcy the Dog

Belle the Dog

Maurice the Cat

Drackie the Cat

Stetson the Stallion

Maggie the Horse

Some Cool Facts About Eagles

1. The bald eagle has been the United States emblem and mascot since 1782.

2. Although an eagle has a wing span up to seven and a half feet, an eagle will only weigh about 9 pounds.

3. Bald eagles are so named since "balde" is an Old English word that simply means "white".

4. Bald eagles mate for life.

5. Bald eagles can swim.

6. Bald eagles usually live near a body of water since their favorite food to hunt is fish.

7. A bald eagle will get his white plumage in about 4 to 5 years.

8. If you hear a bald eagle's scream on tv, it's usually a hawk. Bald eagles make more of a chirpping sound.

9. Bald eagles are found only in North America.

10. In the nest, the female bald eagle will lay one to three eggs. She will incubate (sit on) the eggs for 34 to 36 days.

Advanced Learners
The 20 Words

1. **Autumn:** The time of year usually in October and November when the leaves start to change.
2. **Coincidentally:** When two things happen at the same time but not expected to happen.
3. **Confident:** To be sure that something will happen.
4. **Downcast:** To be sad.
5. **Eagerly:** To be very excited while waiting on something.
6. **Ecstatic:** To be very happy and overjoyed.
7. **Gentleman:** A boy or man who is kind and has good manners.
8. **Grazing Field:** Land where animals eat grass or hay.
9. **Guiding:** Leading the way for someone.
10. **Herding:** To keep a group of animals together.
11. **Introduced:** To have someone meet someone else by their name.
12. **Journey:** To go on a trip or adventure.
13. **Picturesque:** A beautiful place or nice view.
14. **Ruminating:** Thinking.
15. **Search:** To look for something or someone.
16. **Sincerely:** To be honest and truthful.
17. **Soaring:** Something flying in the sky.
18. **Stumbled:** To trip when walking or moving.
19. **Tranquil:** To be calm and peaceful.
20. **Unison:** Doing something together with someone else.

www.ingramcontent.com/pod-product-compliance
Lightning Source LLC
LaVergne TN
LVHW070048070526
838201LV00036B/358